PUGET SOUND
Educational Service District
601 20th Street East
Fife, WA 98424-1704
(253) 926-5815
1-800-664-4549

THE

AMERICAN

INDIAN

AS

FARMER

By Loverne Morris

Illustrated by Henry Luhrs

Melmont Publishers, Inc
Chicago, Illinois

To my grandchildren: Cathy, Jimmie, Phebe, and Charlie
Fritz; Larry, Terri, Leigh Anna, and Cindy Morris.

The author's thanks go to the following people
for their generous help: Dr. M. R. Harrington, Ella
Robinson, and Bruce Bryan of the Southwest Museum;
Robert Marshall, research librarian, California Institute
of Technology, Southern Branch; Tom Humphrey and
Lillian Deer of the Indian Center, Los Angeles; Indian
lecturer, W. H. H. Pilcher; Margaret Fulmer, Librarian,
Whittier Public Library; and Whittier College Librarian,
Benjamin Whitten.

Library of Congress Catalog Card Number 63-7009

/494

Copyright © 1963 by Melmont Publishers, Incorporated, Chicago, Illinois
All rights reserved
Lithographed in the United States of America

TABLE OF CONTENTS   Pages

A NOTE FROM THE AUTHOR

We usually think of the early American Indians as hunters rather than as farmers. However, long before the white man reached American shores, the Indians were growing some of the same foods we raise today.

U. P. Hedrick, in his **History of Horticulture in America to 1860**, tells us the Cherokees were the best farmers of the Southeast, the Iroquois of the Northeast, while the Mandans were the best plains farmers.

The crop grown most extensively was maize. We call it corn. The Indians were the first people to grow maize. They also raised beans, pumpkins, and squashes. Among their other crops were peanuts, potatoes, sweet potatoes, peppers, and tomatoes.

The Indians were food gatherers before they were farmers. They picked the wild berries that grew in the woods. They gathered seeds from wild plants and ground them into flour or meal for bread. A few Indians, wiser than the rest, no doubt noticed that plants grew from seeds accidentally dropped. After that they saved seeds each year and planted them in gardens near their homes.

One tribe learned from another how to grow various crops. This meant the people had more to eat for it was not always easy to find enough food growing wild. And the men often returned from the hunt empty handed.

The Indians knew their country. Experience taught them which plants could be grown in the warm south and which could withstand the colder northern climate. They learned to cultivate the soil and to fertilize it. Much of this knowledge the Indians passed on to the early settlers.

In making their tools, the Indians used things near at hand. Indians of the shore used shells for hoes and knives. Indians of the hills used flint. Those who lived where deer and buffalo roamed used bone. All Indians used wood. Many made baskets from grasses and the stems of plants. Most used bags they made from the skins and hides of animals. They made jars and dishes from clay.

Indians worked hard in those days to feed and clothe and house their families just as parents do today. This book can tell you about only a few of the hundreds of Indian tribes that farmed the land.

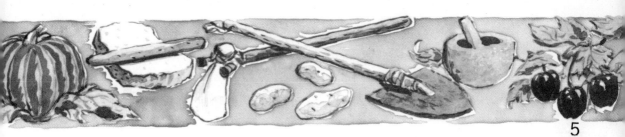

TWO HIDATSA WOMEN RAISE CORN

The day was hot and Otter had been hoeing in her corn field since daybreak. Now the sun was high in the sky. Otter wiped her wet forehead and leaned on her heavy hoe to rest. The hoe was a blade made from the shoulder bone of a buffalo tied to a wooden handle.

Otter was a Hidatsa Indian woman of the Sioux folk who lived in what is today western Minnesota. Her corn, now three inches high, had been planted when the wild gooseberries put out new leaves in spring. Otter had made small mounds into which she dropped the kernels of corn. Spring was the time to plant. Summer was the time to hoe.

Swift Fawn had corn growing in the next field. She was digging with a stick taken from an ash tree. It had been sliced to a sharp edge on one end. Swift Fawn was getting ready to plant beans between her rows of corn. She stopped and straightened her aching back.

"Look! Here comes a trader," she said. "See his pack? He must be the Shawnee who has come this way before."

"Kou-e (hello)," called the stranger.

"Kou-e," returned the women.

The Shawnee had shell beads to trade for corn.

"You have nice fields," he said. "I do not remember their being here when I passed this way before."

"They are new fields," said Otter. "Grandfather killed the trees that grew here by cutting a deep ring around each trunk. After he had chopped them down and burned them, we mixed the ashes with the soil to make it richer."

"Do you have corn to trade?" asked the Shawnee.

"We have corn. Come." Otter led the stranger to a pit between the fields and the village.

The pit, shaped like a huge jug, had both a log cover and one made of skin. Then there was a top cover of earth and ashes. This Otter scraped aside. The floor of the pit was made of willow sticks. The walls were lined with dry grass.

Otter climbed into the pit and brought out a bag of corn for the trader. That left only a little corn and a few bags of beans in the pit. But there would be more after the harvest.

The exchange was made. Otter had her shell beads.
The trader had his corn.

"It is time for food," said Otter. "Will you come
and eat?" She led the way to the side of the field
where stood a leafy tent. This was the cooking tent.

To make the tent, small willow trees had been put
in the ground in a circle. Their tops tied together
formed a roof. In the center of the tent was the
cooking fire.

Otter made some corn bread which she served the
trader along with some dried meat. Having eaten, the
man said his thanks and went on his way.

All summer long the women worked in the fields. At harvest time they had fine corn. The first milk corn was boiled and eaten. The perfect ears were kept for seed to plant the following spring. The rest of the corn the women husked then dried the ears on a platform.

Swift Fawn brought an old tepee cover. This the women tied upside down under the platform and threshed the corn into it. They beat the ears of corn with sticks until the kernels flew off. The kernels were then put into baskets and tossed up and down to blow away the chaff.

Some of the corn was pounded into meal and put into skin bags. The bags of meal and the rest of the corn were stored in the pit.

Now let winter snow and sleet cover the land! There would be food for the hungry families.

SQUASHES GROWN BY SOME MANDANS

Spotted Dove knelt as she patted wet grass onto a strip of old buffalo fur. She was getting kaku-i seeds ready to plant while her friend, Red Swallow, watched. The two women were Mandan Indians. They lived in a village which today would be in North Dakota.

The Mandans called their soft-shelled squashes kaku-i. They also grew hard-shelled squashes, corn, and beans.

Spotted Dove mixed sage and buckbrush leaves with the wet squash seeds. Spreading the mixture on the grass mat on the fur, she folded the whole to make a bundle. To keep it warm, she hung the bundle on a pole near the fire in the lodge. The warmth and dampness would make the seeds sprout. Then the plants would grow fast.

12

"Come and help me make a scarecrow," said Red Swallow. "The birds have been after my young corn. We will make a big scarecrow for the middle of my field."

The two women gathered sticks from the bushes by the river. They drove two tall sticks into the ground for legs. They tied on two sticks for arms and used a ball of fur for the head. Then a belted dress of buckskin and the scarecrow was finished.

"Now, when the wind waves the dress, the crows will be afraid to eat the tender leaves of my corn plants," said Red Swallow. "Let's make a scarecrow for your field, Spotted Dove."

One morning Spotted Dove said to Red Swallow. "My kaku·i have sprouted. They are ready to plant. I have more than I need. You may have some."

Each woman had two rows of corn and two rows of beans. Each now planted squash seeds between the rows of corn and beans. The mounds were smaller than the corn hills. The sprouted seeds were planted in the sides of the mounds so rain could not form a crust of dirt over them.

All during the hot summer Spotted Dove and Red Swallow tended their fields. The squashes were ready to harvest before the corn was ripe.

The two women gathered their squashes in baskets. They cooked what their families could eat at once, then dried the rest. Sitting with robes in their laps, they sliced the squashes with knives made of bone. The slices were stuck onto sticks to dry.

When the squash slices were dry, Spotted Dove and Red Swallow took them off the sticks and strung them on strings made of grasses. For this they used a wooden needle. Some of the strings they looped over sticks that rested on forked poles in their lodges. Some they put into sacks made of skin. There would be enough dried squash to last through the long, hard, winter.

EARLY WESTERN IRRIGATION DITCHES

Long before white men came to America, the Indians, living in what are now the Salt and Gila River valleys in Arizona, had learned to irrigate their corn and cotton fields. Very little rain falls in this part of the country. The first canals may have started as ditches made by flood waters when streams overflowed their banks in the spring. Some of the ditch water running into nearby fields helped the crops grow faster. But most of the time the ditches were dry.

The Indians found that by putting a dam across a nearby river, water could be made to flow into the ditches even during the dry season.

Scientists who have studied the way of life of the red men say the early dams were made of poles and brush and stone.

First the Indians drove a row of stakes across the river near a ditch. Then they threw in brush and branches which were carried down against the stakes by the current. Baskets filled with stones were rolled against the brush and branches to make the dam. The dam held back the water so that it could be made to flow into the old, dry ditch.

With wooden digging sticks and crude wooden shovels, the Indians made a canal out of the ditch. They called it the mother canal. They dug it deeper and longer. They lined it with clay. The canal passed many fields. A small ditch led from the mother canal into each man's fields.

Many of the early canals were as much as seven feet deep and four feet wide at the bottom. The sides were built like steps making the canal much wider at the top.

Someone was always on hand to keep an eye on the water. The guard stayed in a little house near the canal where he could watch the ditches. Water might start to run into a gopher hole. This had to be stopped. Perhaps an Indian tried to take water for his field before it was his turn. This could not be allowed. The guard saw that each man got water in his turn.

Water gates of wood stopped the flow of water. The gates could be raised to let water flow into the fields or lowered to keep the water out. The fields were edged with ridges so that the irrigation water would not run away.

These canal builders finally left their canals and moved away. Some were routed by conquering armies. Some kept losing their crops to raiding tribes who did not bother to farm.

It is thought that many of the Indians moved away to find better land and better water. The Indians knew that much salt is bad for crops. Scientists say that the Gila and Salt rivers do contain some salt. Canals leading from them could in time have become encrusted with salt.

For several hundred years the canals were dry and unused. They were rediscovered and now some of them carry water for today's farmers.

GROWING COTTON IN THE VERDE RIVER VALLEY

Blue Feather and Yucca lived in a house of rock and mud that stood on a ledge above their father's fields. Blue Feather and Yucca were Sinagua Indian boys of the Verde River Valley in what is now Arizona. In early spring they had helped their father plant corn and beans, squashes and pumpkins. Late spring was the time to plant the cotton.

Although it was a land of little rain, crops grew well in the valley. This was because irrigation ditches brought water from Beaver Creek to the people's fields.

When the cotton seeds were in the ground, Father said to the boys, "Today I want you to bring rocks so that I can build up the edges of the field. The water must be kept inside so it will soak into the ground."

Like the other farmers in the area, Father built the ridge of rocks and dirt all around his field. When it was his turn to get water from the mother ditch, he put a wooden water gate across the ditch. This sent the water flowing into the little ditch that led into his

own fields. He let the water run for three days to let the water soak down into the ground. Then he blocked off his little ditch so that his neighbors could get water for their fields.

At harvest time Blue Feather and Yucca helped gather the crops. They picked the cotton from the bolls and straightened the fibers with their fingers.

To remove the seeds, the cotton was spread between blankets. It was then beaten with sticks until backs ached and arms were tired and sore.

Next came more hard work. The cotton had to be rolled and pulled and twisted, then pulled and twisted and rolled into coarse thread. Then the thread was dyed many different colors after which it was ready to be woven into capes and blankets.

Mother had been saving turkey feathers for a long time. Now Father wove the feathers and the cotton thread into capes for everyone in the family. Blue Feather's cape was blue. Yucca's was a pretty yellow. There was a bright red cape for Baby Sister.

DRY FARMING AMONG THE HOPI

Paho and Makewa were dry farmers. They could raise crops on land so dry that one might think nothing would grow there. They lived in Oraibi, a pueblo, or town, on the edge of a mesa in Arizona. Mesa is the Hopi Indians' word for a flat-topped hill.

The people of Oraibi planted and tended their crops as they had always been tended and planted by the Hopi.

In the early morning clouds sailed high in the blue, blue sky. Paho and Makewa, together with other men of the pueblo, climbed down the many stone steps that led to their fields in the valley below.

CASCADE VIEW SCHOOL LIBRARY

"We will stir the soil into a thick blanket of dust. Then the top will not crack and let the sun suck the dampness from the earth back into the sky." It was Makewa who spoke as the men moved down the rows, working side by side.

The beans were planted in holes three inches deep. Because the field lay between two hills, or mesas, storm winds would not blow away the dust blanket.

"The moon is new. That is the time to plant our beans," said Paho.

"That is right," said the others. "Now is the time." Each man carried a bag of white seed beans. "We will plant the beans deep. Their roots must reach every drop of water the land still holds from the winter rains."

25

After the beans had been planted, the men hoed their corn and weeded around the spreading squash plants. For hoes they used shoulder blades of the deer fastened to wooden handles.

"Rabbits have been feasting in the fields," said Paho. The men lost no time in setting basket traps. When Mr. Rabbit walked in, a door would close behind him and he would be caught in the trap.

During most of the long, dry summer the fields looked happy.

"The young wind walks in the corn field and the green leaves dance," said Makewa.

But then the corn began to droop as a blazing sun scorched the land. "We must have a prayer ceremony," said the people of Oraibi. "We must ask the Sky People to send rain for our crops."

Everyone joined in the rain dance. When the rain fell and the parched fields turned green once more, the Hopi were thankful. Had not the Sky People answered their prayers?

The crops ripened. The harvest was good. "There will be plenty of food for the coming winter," said the people.

The crops were dried on the flat housetops. The ears of corn—red, yellow, blue, and black—looked like piles of bright beads in the sunlight.

The women hung dried ears of corn from the rafters of the houses. Some of the corn they ground between two stones to make meal and flour for the good corn bread the Hopi call piki.

The dried beans were put into big clay pots with tight skin covers. The squashes were dried and stored in baskets.

The harvest had indeed been good!

THE THREE LOVING SISTERS OF THE IROQUOIS

Four women worked in the fields. As they worked they sang:

"The Sky Chief sees our tall corn growing.

He sees our beans embracing the corn.

He sees our squashes and our pumpkins.

He sees and blesses our golden sunflowers."

These were Cayuga women of the Ho-De-No-Sau-Nee, which means people of the long house. We call them Iroquois. They lived in what is now upper New York State.

Flying Fingers was hoeing the corn with a curved piece of wood fastened to a long handle. Plum Blossom was busy getting the weeds out of the border of sunflower plants. Quiet Lake and New Moon were sitting on the ground digging the grass from the rows of beans and squashes. They used short sticks for this.

"What would we do without our three loving sisters?" said Flying Fingers. "Corn is the tall sister. Bean likes to lean on her. Squash, the little sister, crawls at their feet. Some nights, when no one is looking, they dance and sing in the starlight."

"I know we could not do without the three sisters," said Plum Blossom, "but sunflower is important, too. When her seeds are ripe, I pound them into meal or use them to make oil for cooking."

"We all do," said New Moon, "and sunflower seed meal is hard to make."

"That is because it takes time," said Flying Fingers. "Some of our women do not take time to do things right. Some do not soak the corn seeds before planting them. I always soak mine in medicine water made from reed grass and roots of bottlebrush grass. This keeps the worms and birds from eating the seeds after they have been planted. Soaking also helps the sprouts break through the kernel's tough skin."

"I dampened my squash seeds before planting them," said New Moon. I filled a bark box with old wood from a rotted stump. I put the wet squash seeds into it and kept it near the fire until the seeds sprouted."

The sunflowers grew in a border around the edge of the field. Plum blossom had planted them before the corn was put into the ground. Seeds of the climbing beans had been planted in pockets in the sides of the corn hills.

The men built a fence of stakes around the fields to keep out the deer. Flying Fingers made a whistle from a hollow stick and swung it from a pole. When the wind blew through the stick, it made a whistling sound. This frightened the birds away from the fields.

At harvest time the women dried the sunflower heads, the beans, and the squashes on a drying platform before storing them for winter use. Some of the fresh, new corn was boiled or roasted for a special treat. The ripe ears were husked then put into a crib, or bin.

The corn crib stood on four posts. The sides were made of crossed poles so air could get to the corn. A roof over the crib protected the corn from rain and snow. There are farmers who still make the same kind of corn crib as that used by the Cayuga Indians so long ago.

POTATOES COME TO THE ALGONQUIANS

Shooting Star stood in the doorway of her wigwam late one spring evening. She was watching Quiet Owl as he hurried along the path leading from the beach where a ship lay at anchor. A heavy bag bobbed up and down on his back. It was plain to see he was excited.

Shooting Star and Quiet Owl were Algonquian Indians. They lived in Secota Village in what is now Virginia.

Once he had reached the wigwam, Quiet Owl pulled his wife inside. He dug down into the bag and brought out what looked like a fat, brown root.

"What is it?" asked Shooting Star.

"An openauk. I have a bagful of the things. The white men on the ship in the harbor gave them to me. The men learned about them from Indians beyond the southern seas. The ship's men say the openauk is good to eat when cooked. Let's cook one and try it."

Quiet Owl called the thing in his hand an openauk. We would call it a potato.

Shooting Star boiled the potato by dropping hot stones into a clay pot of water. Then she and Quiet Owl tasted the new food. They found it good.

"Will you tell the people?" Shooting Star asked.

"Now is not the time," said Quiet Owl. "The white men said to cut each openauk into pieces, leaving an eye in each piece. Then I am to plant two pieces to a hole. See the eyes? A sprout will grow from each eye."

That very night, by firelight, Shooting Star and Quiet Owl cut the potatoes into pieces. At dawn, before their neighbors were yet about, Quiet Owl planted the pieces in the garden beside the corn and beans, the pumpkins and the sunflowers. Shooting Star added a gourdful of water to each hole and covered the potato pieces with little hills of dirt.

At last sprouts pushed through the earth where the potatoes had been planted. Rain and sun helped them grow. The villagers watched and waited and whispered. They had never seen any plants quite like these.

"Poison," said some. "Quiet Owl, why do you tend the poison plants so carefully?"

Quiet Owl smiled and was silent as he hoed between the rows of potato plants. Harvest time came. The leaves of the plants turned brown. The stems turned yellow. The villagers shook their heads.

"Before sunrise tomorrow we will dig in the openauk patch," Quiet Owl said to Shooting Star.

Somehow the villagers knew the secret would soon be out. As he started to dig, Quiet Owl saw the neighbors coming to watch. He put his wooden spade into a potato hill. He lifted out five potatoes. He dug into another hill and added six potatoes to the pile. Some were egg-sized, others only the size of a walnut.

A neighbor picked up a potato and looked at it carefully. "What is it? What is it for?" he asked.

"It is an openauk. It is good to cook and to eat." Quiet Owl told how he had been given the potatoes by the men on the ship.

Shooting Star boiled some of the potatoes. She baked some in hot ashes. She and Quiet Owl ate some to show they were not poison. Then all the people tasted the potatoes.

"Good!" they said.

"I will save half of them for seed. We will all plant pieces of openauk," said Quiet Owl.

And from then on the people of Secota Village had potatoes to eat.

PEANUTS AND SWEET POTATOES RAISED
BY THE CREEKS

Fat Raccoon, his wife Moonstone, and their young son Sandbird were Creek Indians. They lived where Georgia touches the Atlantic Ocean. Their village of wigwams lay between the forest and the shore. The people's sunny gardens were on the forest side of the village. Everywhere birds flashed from sunshine to shadow among the bright blossoms and dark leaves. The birds were as gay and colorful as the blossoms.

Today the family was going to plant their sweet potatoes and peanuts. Sandbird liked nothing better than to be taken to the gardens. He was just a little boy but he could help. Mother let him carry some peanuts in a basket of his own. Her basket was a big cone with a flat bottom. She carried it full of sweet potatoes on her back. Father carried a digging stick and a hoe. The hoe was a big sea shell tied onto the end of a stick.

The sweet potatoes were about the size of Sandbird's fist. Fat Raccoon planted them in wet sand in a sunny corner of the garden. Moonstone and Sandbird planted the peanuts. Moonstone made rows of little hills. Sandbird dropped three or four peanuts into each hill. The planting took almost all day.

As soon as the sweet potatoes sprouted, they were taken from their bed of sand and planted in hills as the peanuts had been. All summer long Mother hoed them and the rows of corn and beans and pumpkins. Father hoed the tobacco.

On the first nippy fall morning Fat Raccoon said, "Today we will dig the sweet potatoes. We must not wait until the frost spoils them."

The sweet potatoes were dried on a rack under a roof made of palm branches. They were then stored in a dugout for winter use.

Fat Raccoon made the dugout. First he propped a sloping roof against short posts. He dug a hole underneath, piling the dirt on top of the roof. He knew sweet potatoes are hard to keep and must not get too hot or too cold.

The peanut plants had bloomed during the summer, the blossom stalks had turned downward and nosed into the dirt. The peanut pods developed underground. When the pods were ripe, Moonstone pulled up the plants and turned them upside-down to start the drying. Later the plants were put on a rack so the peanuts could be picked from the vines more easily.

The peanuts we buy today have been roasted. The Indians also roasted their peanuts many years ago. Moonstone roasted hers in a clay oven heated with hot coals or stones or with ashes from the fireplace. She also broke some of the shelled nuts into small bits. These she boiled to make a hot drink.

Sandbird thought there was nothing quite so good as peanut butter spread on the crisp corn bread his mother baked on a hot stone in the cooking hut.

To make the peanut butter, Moonstone cleaned out the hollow in the top of a stump. Into the hollow she put the peanuts, then pounded and pounded them with the rounded end of a short club.

TOMATOES AND PEPPERS IN A TUMUCUAN GARDEN

"There are baby tomatls on the tomatl plants, Mother! Come and see!" Little Alligator tugged at his mother's hand as she came out of their thatch-and-reed house. She followed her eager young son to their garden.

Little Alligator and South Wind were Tumucuan Indians. Their home was an island off the southern tip of what is now Florida.

"Look! Do you see the little tomatls? We will have many tomatls to eat, won't we, Mother? When will they be ripe?"

What Little Alligator called tomatls, we now know as tomatoes. For a long time our ancestors were afraid to eat this delicious fruit thinking it was poison. But the Indians knew better.

Little Alligator had helped plant the tomatls. First the seeds had been sprouted in a seed bed. Later the young plants had been put in rows in the ground. As the plants grew tall they were tied to stakes. Now, strong and healthy, they were beginning to bear fruit.

Corn and beans, sweet potatoes and peppers also grew in South Wind's garden. The pepper plants looked very much like the tomatl plants except that the leaves of the pepper plants were smooth, not hairy. Later in the summer there would be sweet, round green peppers and pointed, hot red peppers that we call chili peppers.

Because the weather on the island was never very cold, South Wind could grow crops in winter as well as summer. During the hot summer days she and Little Alligator wore big straw hats to protect them from the sun as they worked in the garden. Father was away fishing with the other men most of the time.

When harvest time came, Little Alligator had all the tomatls he could eat. There were round, red cherry tomatoes and small, pear-shaped ones. Little Alligator liked to pick them from the vines and suck the warm juice.

South Wind cooked some of the tomatls and beans with the peppers. If she wanted a hot, spicy food, she left the pepper seeds in. If not, she took out the seeds. She used the pointed, red peppers to make a powder much like our chili powder. She dried the peppers then ground them by pounding them in a wooden bowl with a wooden hammer.

Since she could raise crops all during the year, South Wind did not have to store as much food as did the northern Indians. She did dry some of the beans she raised. These she put into a shelter that looked like a little thatched house on poles. Sweet potatoes were also stored in the shelter. Some of her corn, South Wind ground into meal for bread.

"There will be food for many a fine feast when your father comes home with fish from the bay," the woman told her son.

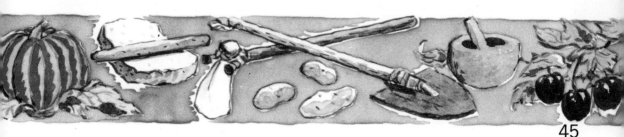

INDEX

Born in Lyon County, Kansas, Loverne Morris grew up in Emporia across the street from William Allen White. From him she early acquired an interest in creative writing. After a brief interval of teaching, she came to California where she met and married Herbert I. Morris who shares her interest in good writing. Their two children grew up surrounded by books. The bedtime stories created for this son and daughter were the first things written by Mrs. Morris to appear in print. They and a few of her other stories were published in farm, home, and children's magazines.

Loverne Morris entered the newspaper field in 1941. Since then she has done most kinds of news reporting. In recent years she has done local history features for the Daily News of Whittier, California.

Mrs. Morris divides her time between her home in the hills near Whittier and a cabin in the San Gabriel Mountains. She has made friends with raccoons, deer, chipmunks, and foxes and fed many birds of the wild. Indian life has long interested her, and the finding of an ancient metaté affords a real thrill.

Henry Luhrs, a Californian by birth, actually has not spent too much time in his native state. His work as a free lance illustrator has taken him both to New York and Chicago.

Mr. Luhrs' illustrations have appeared in such magazines as Cosmopolitan, Colliers, and Red Book. He has also illustrated a number of children's books for the Whitman Publishing Company of Racine, Wisconsin.

Mr. Luhrs received his art training at the California Institute of Art in San Francisco, as well as the Art League and Grand Central Art School in New York. At present he and Mrs. Luhrs make their home in Laguna Beach, California.

CASCADE VIEW SCHOOL LIBRARY

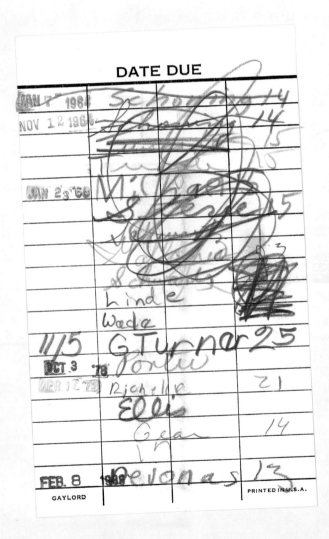

DATE DUE

JAN 1 1964	Schocking		14
NOV 12 1964			14
			5
JAN 23 '68	Michael		5
			3
	Linda		
	Wade		
11/5	G Turner		25
OCT 3 '73	Portie		
APR 17 '73	Richelle		21
	Elli		
	Gea		14
FEB. 8 196	Devonas		13
GAYLORD			PRINTED IN U.S.A.